TESSA BRAMLEY

Traditional Puddings

Tessa Bramley

Traditional Puddings

Photography by Simon Wheeler

WEIDENFELD & NICOLSON

Tessa Bramley

Tessa Bramley is chef-patron of the highly acclaimed Old Vicarage restaurant in the village of Ridgway, outside Sheffield. Her innovative modern menus mix British and Mediterranean influences with some from even further afield, and have earned her high marks in *The Good Food Guide*. In 1995 the Old Vicarage was awarded two stars by the *Egon Ronay Guide*: one of only six restaurants outside London to achieve this status.

Tessa is a regular presenter on Channel 4's series *Here's One I Made Earlier*. She was a featured chef in Robert Carrier's series which was broadcast as a strand on ITV's *This Morning*. Tessa is a self-taught chef and her first book, *The Instinctive Cook*, was published in 1995.

Contents

Blessed be he that invented pudding...

oh what an excellent thing

is an English pudding!

To come in pudding-time

is as much as to say to

come in the most lucky moment

in the world.

H. MISSON DE VALBOURG
(A French visitor to Britain in 1690)

Introduction

British traditional puddings – sometimes elaborate, often delicate and elegant; baked, boiled or steamed; fools, tarts, trifles and crumbles – are an essential part of our culinary heritage, a part which is the envy of the world. Puddings have been regarded as one of the glories of British cooking, and they are an indulgence to be revelled in.

Wild and cottage garden fruits have often formed a basis for our puddings and in these days of healthy eating, when puddings are served in small amounts or only occasionally, it is even more important to use the freshest and best ingredients available. Free-range eggs, unsalted butter, clotted cream and wild flower honeys give a true taste of British style; don't be tempted to substitute low-fat and reduced sugar products.

Finish the meal with a flourish and give your guests a memorable and irresistible treat.

Note: I have used size 1 or extra-large eggs in all these recipes.

Tessa Brawley

Summer puddings

SERVES 4

175 g/6 oz blackcurrants
175 g/6 oz redcurrants
175 g/6 oz blueberries or
    bilberries
175 g/6 oz small strawberries
175 g/6 oz raspberries
175 g/6 oz cherries, pitted
4–6 tablespoons caster sugar
1 lemon, zest pared in large
    strips
1 large loaf of stoneground
    wholemeal bread, thinly
    sliced, crusts removed
mint leaves and icing sugar,
    to decorate

Begin making the puddings the day before you need them. Reserve a few little bunches of berries for decoration, then strip the stalks and hulls from all the fruit. Place the fruit in a saucepan with 4 tablespoons of the sugar and the strips of lemon zest. Heat gently, until the juices just begin to flow from the fruit, then remove from the heat. Taste and add more sugar if necessary. Pour the fruit into a colander set over a bowl to collect the juices. Remove the lemon zest.

Cut out four circles of bread to fit the bases of four individual pudding moulds. Cut strips of bread long enough to line the sides of the moulds with about 5 mm/¼ inch over. Dip the bread in the fruit juice, then line the moulds, putting the circles in first and then pressing the strips up the sides. Pack the fruit into the moulds, right to the top of the bread. Cut four more circles of bread to cover the fruit, first dipping them in the fruit juice. Cover with cling film and place on a small tray. Cover with another tray and press it in place with heavy weights. Chill overnight.

Purée any remaining fruit with its juices, pass through a fine sieve into a container and chill.

Before serving, trim away any excess bread. Run a thin-bladed knife around each pudding and invert on to a serving plate. Shake to remove the puddings from the moulds. Pour a little sauce over and around each pudding, and decorate with the reserved berries and some small mint leaves. Dust lightly with icing sugar. Serve with pouring cream crème fraîche.

Chargrilled fillet of cod with pesto and a rocket salad is a lovely dish to precede a classic summer pudding.

RASPBERRY QUEEN OF PUDDINGS

SERVES 4–6

50 g/2 oz fresh white
   breadcrumbs
grated zest of 1 lemon
600 ml/1 pint hot vanilla custard
   (page 34)
3 tablespoons raspberry jam
175 g/6 oz raspberries, washed
   and dried

Meringue
5 egg whites
a pinch of salt
4 tablespoons caster sugar
1 tablespoon flaked almonds
   (optional)

Raspberry coulis
175 g/6 oz raspberries
50 g/2 oz icing sugar

Sprinkle the breadcrumbs and grated lemon zest into a 1 litre/1¾ pint ovenproof serving dish and pour the hot custard over. Leave to cool, then chill in the refrigerator for 2 hours.

Preheat the oven to 120°C/250°F/Gas Mark ½.

Warm the jam with 1 tablespoon cold water. Pass through a fine sieve to remove the seeds, then spread the jam over the custard and top with the raspberries.

To make the meringue, whisk the egg whites in a bowl with a pinch of salt, until they form stiff peaks. Whisk in 3 tablespoons of the sugar and whisk to form stiff, glossy peaks.

Pile the meringue on top of the raspberries in rough peaks – do not attempt to spread the meringue, but make certain the raspberries are completely covered. Scatter the remaining sugar and the flaked almonds over the meringue. Bake for 25–30 minutes, until the meringue is crisp with lightly golden peaks.

Meanwhile, make the coulis: toss the raspberries in the icing sugar, then press through a sieve to remove the seeds.

Serve the pudding hot or cold, with the raspberry coulis.

As a main course, how about a summery fish dish such as baked red mullet with a tomato and chilli salsa?

Rhubarb and ginger fool

SERVES 4

150 ml/5 fl oz double cream
1 teaspoon icing sugar
2 pieces of stem ginger
600 g/1¼ lb early season forced
   rhubarb
225 g/8 oz caster sugar
2–3 drops of pink food colouring
   (optional)
150 ml/5 fl oz vanilla custard
   (page 34), chilled

Whisk the cream with the icing sugar until firm, but not stiff and dry. Chill.

Slice the ginger thinly and then slice across into thin strips.

Top, tail and wash the rhubarb, leaving the pink skin on. Put the rhubarb in a wide shallow pan with the caster sugar and 3 tablespoons water, and simmer until softened to a pulp. If the colour is not pink enough from the skins, add two or three drops of colouring (it should be pale pink, but as the rhubarb gets older the purée will be less pink and may need a little help).

Press the purée through a very coarse sieve, just to remove any stringy bits but leaving some texture in the fruit. Stir in the ginger and chill well.

Place alternate spoonfuls of the custard, cream and fruit purée in a wide bowl. Using a spatula, draw them lightly together to make a marbled fool. Spoon into glasses to show off the marbled effect, and serve with hazelnut shortbread fingers (page 35).

A gutsy February dish of braised oxtail with mashed potatoes would be a perfect foil for this light fool made with the new season's rhubarb.

GOOSEBERRY AND ELDERFLOWER CRUMBLE

SERVES 4–6

butter for preparing the dish
900 g/2 lb gooseberries
4 heads (umbels) of elderflowers
225 g/8 oz caster sugar
175 g/6 oz plain flour
a pinch of salt
85 g/3 oz unsalted butter,
    chilled and diced
25 g/1 oz hazelnuts (or
    cobnuts), chopped

Preheat the oven to 200°C/400°F/Gas Mark 6.
Butter a 1.2 litre/2 pint ovenproof shallow dish.

Top and tail the gooseberries and put them in the dish.
Gently wash the elderflowers and shake dry, holding
them upside down to remove any insects. Sprinkle
150 g/5 oz of the sugar over the gooseberries and tuck
the elderflowers among the fruit.

Sift the flour and salt into a mixing bowl and rub in
the butter until it resembles fine breadcrumbs. Stir in
the remaining sugar and the chopped nuts.

Beginning at the outer edges (which helps to prevent
the juices from rising up the sides), spoon the topping
evenly over the fruit. Firm the crumbs down with the
back of the spoon and then mark lines with a fork to
help make the top crisp.

Bake for 40–45 minutes, until the top is crisp and
golden brown and the gooseberries tender. Serve hot
or cold, with custard or crème fraîche.

*A light fish dish such as sea bass roasted over fennel with
roasted vegetables would be an excellent main course to precede
this early summer dessert.*

STRAWBERRY AND ROSE PETAL SHORTCAKES

SERVES 6

225 g/8 oz unsalted butter
125 g/4 oz vanilla-flavoured
    caster sugar
225 g/8 oz plain flour
125 g/4 oz semolina

Rose cream
2 teaspoons lemon juice
3 large red old-fashioned
    scented roses*
300 ml/10 fl oz double cream
1 tablespoon icing sugar, sifted
½ teaspoon rosewater

Filling and decoration
450g/1 lb ripe strawberries,
    sliced
crystallized rose petals (page 37)
sprigs of mint

** Pick the rose petals in the
morning on a dry day and
examine them carefully for
insects before use. Do not use
roses that have been sprayed
with insecticide.*

Cream the butter and vanilla sugar together in a large bowl until pale and fluffy. Sieve the flour and semolina together, then gradually work into the creamed mixture. Finish the mixing with your hands, then gently knead on a lightly floured surface until smooth. Roll out quite thinly and prick with a fork. Using a fluted cutter about 8 cm/3 inches in diameter, cut out two circles for each shortcake and lift on to a lightly floured baking sheet. Chill for about 30 minutes; this helps the shortcakes to retain their shape. Preheat the oven to 180°C/350°F/Gas Mark 4.

To make the rose cream, place the lemon juice in a bowl, crush the rose petals in your hand and drop them into the lemon juice. Turn the petals gently in the juice to keep their colour bright. Add the cream, icing sugar and rosewater, stir to blend, then leave in a cool place for 30 minutes for the flavours to infuse the cream.

Bake the shortcakes in the oven for 10–12 minutes, until just tinged golden (they will become crisp only when cold). Using a palette knife, lift on to a wire rack and leave to cool.

Strain the cream through a sieve, discarding the petals. Whisk the cream until firm but not stiff.

To assemble the shortcakes, spread half the circles fairly thickly with rose cream, top with sliced strawberries and then with the second layer of shortbread. Top with some crystallized rose petals and a sprig of mint.

A fragrant dessert for summer entertaining. Why not begin with poached wild salmon with mayonnaise, new potatoes and a herby green salad?

BAKED CHOCOLATE PUDDING
with hot chocolate fudge sauce

SERVES 4

100 g/3½ oz self-raising flour
½ level teaspoon baking powder
¼ level teaspoon bicarbonate of
  soda
1 rounded tablespoon cocoa
  powder
70 g/2½ oz caster sugar
1 extra-large egg, beaten
1 tablespoon golden syrup
100 ml/3½ fl oz milk
100 ml/3½ fl oz sunflower oil

Chocolate fudge sauce

25 g/1 oz unsalted butter
85 g/3 oz extra bitter dark
  chocolate (Meunier or
  Valrhona)
200 ml/7 fl oz double cream
225 g/8 oz icing sugar, sifted

To serve

vanilla custard (page 34)

Preheat the oven to 150°C/300°F/Gas Mark 2. Grease four individual 175 ml/6 fl oz pudding moulds.

Sift the flour, baking powder, bicarbonate of soda, cocoa and caster sugar together into a mixing bowl. Make a well in the centre. Pour the egg into the well with the golden syrup, milk and oil. Gradually draw the dry ingredients in from the sides of the bowl and beat to make a smooth batter.

Pour into the prepared moulds and bake in the oven for about 30 minutes, until springy to the touch.

To make the sauce, melt the butter, chocolate and cream together in a double boiler. Gradually beat in the icing sugar until glossy.

To serve, unmould the puddings on to four dessert plates and pour the fudge sauce over and around the puddings. Pour hot custard around the edges of the plates and – using the point of a small knife or a wooden skewer – draw the custard and fudge sauce together in a swirling movement.

Although appearing to be rich, this pudding is actually very light and would make a good second course to follow a simple chicken dish, maybe cooked with lemon, ginger and coriander.

MADEIRA TIPSY TRIFLE

SERVES 6-8

vanilla custard (page 34)
225 g/8 oz raspberries and 2
   tablespoons icing sugar or
   200 g/7 oz canned apricots,
   drained, and the juice of
   ½ lemon
150 ml/5 fl oz Madeira
2 tablespoons fresh orange juice
1 tablespoon brandy
3 tablespoons caster sugar
1 layer of orange sandwich cake
   (page 36), or plain sponge
   cake or sponge fingers
2-3 tablespoons good-quality
   raspberry or apricot jam
1 tablespoon flaked almonds,
   toasted, to decorate

Chantilly cream

1 vanilla pod
450 ml/15 fl oz double cream
2 heaped teaspoons icing sugar,
   sifted

First, assemble all the parts. Make the custard. Mix the raspberries and sugar together in a bowl, then press through a sieve to remove the seeds. Alternatively, purée the apricots and sharpen the taste with a little lemon juice.

Mix the Madeira, orange juice, brandy and caster sugar together, taste and add more sugar if necessary.

For the Chantilly cream, split the vanilla pod and scoop the seeds into the cream. Add the icing sugar and whisk together lightly to form a soft, spreadable consistency.

Slice the sponge in half horizontally, spread thickly with the jam, and sandwich the layers back together. Cut into pieces and arrange in a glass dish. Pour over enough of the Madeira mixture to moisten the sponges well.

Top with the fruit purée, then spread with the custard. Spread about two-thirds of the Chantilly cream thickly on top. Whisk the remaining cream until stiff and pipe on to the trifle. Decorate with toasted flaked almonds.

A luxurious trifle is traditionally part of a Christmas high tea. What about rum-roasted gammon, Waldorf salad and some homemade chutney to start?

APPLE AND CINNAMON BROWN BETTY

SERVES 4

butter for preparing the dish
600g/1¼ lb Bramley apples
125 g/4 oz demerara sugar, plus
   1 tablespoon extra
grated zest and juice of 1 lemon
1 cinnamon stick, broken into 5
   or 6 pieces
85g/3 oz unsalted butter
175g/6 oz fresh brown
   breadcrumbs

Preheat the oven to 180°C/350°F/Gas Mark 4.
Butter a 1.2 litre/2 pint ovenproof dish.

Peel, core and thinly slice the apples into a bowl. Mix in the demerara sugar, the zest and juice of the lemon and the broken cinnamon stick.

Melt the butter in a heavy-based frying pan and tip in the breadcrumbs. Cook over a medium heat, stirring constantly with a wooden spoon, until all the butter has been absorbed into the bread and the crumbs have separated out again and are golden in colour.

Layer the apples and crumbs in the buttered dish, finishing with a layer of crumbs. Press down with the back of the spoon and sprinkle the extra tablespoon of demerara sugar on top.

Bake in the centre of the oven for 45–50 minutes, until the apples are soft (test with a skewer) and the top is crisp and brown. If it seems to be getting too brown before the apples are cooked, cover the surface lightly with a piece of baking parchment or foil. Do not tuck it round the dish as this will spoil the crispness of the topping. Serve hot, with clotted cream.

The autumnal flavours of pot-roasted pheasant with tangerine zest and thyme, with roasted parsnips, would be just right before this spicy apple pudding.

Blackberry soufflé

SERVES 4

butter and caster sugar for
    preparing the dishes
500g/1 lb 2 oz fresh ripe
    blackberries
1 teaspoon lemon juice
85 g/3 oz caster sugar
3 egg whites
a pinch of salt
3 tablespoons caster sugar
icing sugar for dusting

Preheat the oven to 200°C/400°F/Gas Mark 6. Lightly butter four individual soufflé dishes and sprinkle a little caster sugar in each. Shake the dishes to coat the insides evenly with caster sugar.

Press the blackberries through a medium sieve into a bowl. Add the lemon juice and caster sugar to the thick purée of blackberries. Taste and add a squeeze more lemon juice if necessary: it should taste very fruity but quite sharp. Chill well.

Put 1 dessertspoon of blackberry purée in the bottom of each soufflé dish.

In a perfectly clean bowl, whisk the egg whites with a pinch of salt, until they form stiff peaks. Fold in half the caster sugar and whisk to form stiff, glossy peaks. Repeat with the remaining sugar.

Using a balloon whisk, carefully fold in the blackberry purée until evenly mixed. Pile into the soufflé dishes. Smooth the sides and top with a palette knife, allowing the mixture to stand about 2 cm/¾ inch above the rims.

Bake until well risen and golden, about 4–5 minutes. Dust with icing sugar and serve immediately. Some blackberry sorbet would be a rather nice accompaniment.

Blackberry soufflé makes a light autumn pudding to follow a traditional roast such as a loin of pork with apple sauce.

CARAMELIZED APPLE TARTS

SERVES 4

1½ teaspoons lemon juice
1 egg
225 g/8 oz plain flour
1 teaspoon icing sugar
½ teaspoon salt
150 g/5 oz unsalted butter,
    chilled and diced
Pastry cream (page 36)

Apple purée

2 Bramley apples, peeled, cored
    and sliced
1½ tablespoons caster sugar
1 strip of lemon zest
1 tablespoon Calvados

Apple topping

40 g/1½ oz butter
1 tablespoon caster sugar
3 Cox's apples, peeled, cored
    and thinly sliced
icing sugar for dusting

To make the pastry, beat the lemon juice and egg with 2 tablespoons iced water, then chill until thickened. Sift the flour, icing sugar and salt into a bowl, then rub in the butter until the mixture resembles breadcrumbs. Add the chilled liquid and stir until the mixture binds to form a loose dough. Turn out and knead lightly until smooth. Wrap and chill for 30 minutes.

Preheat the oven to 190°C/375°F/Gas Mark 5. Roll out one-third of the pastry (chill or freeze the rest for later use) and use to line four individual fluted tart tins. Bake blind for about 20 minutes. Leave to cool.

To make the apple purée, stew the Bramleys gently in a heavy-based pan with the sugar, lemon zest and 1 tablespoon water until the apples collapse and form a dry, thick purée. Add the Calvados, then taste and add a little more sugar if necessary.

Turn the oven to 220°C/425°F/Gas Mark 7.

To make the apple topping, heat the butter and sugar in a saucepan with 1 tablespoon water until dissolved. Bring to the boil. Add the apple slices and cook for 2−3 minutes, until soft and coated with syrup.

Divide the pastry cream between the tart bases and top with 1 tablespoon of apple purée. Overlap the apple slices on top. Bake for 10−12 minutes. If the edges are not golden brown, dredge lightly with icing sugar and caramelize with a blow torch or under a hot grill. To serve, dredge lightly with sifted icing sugar.

Leg of lamb with rosemary and garlic , followed by caramelized apple tart, would be very comforting on a blustery day.

WALNUT AND ORANGE PUDDING
with toffee sauce

SERVES 4

butter for preparing the dish
50 g/2 oz walnuts
50 g/2 oz self-raising flour
¼ teaspoon baking powder
a pinch of salt
125 g/4 oz unsalted butter,
    softened
125 g/4 oz soft brown sugar
grated zest of 1 orange
2 eggs, beaten

Toffee sauce
50 g/2 oz walnuts
85 g/3 oz caster sugar
150 ml/5 fl oz double cream
50 g/2 oz unsalted butter

Preheat the oven to 160°C/325°F/Gas Mark 3.
Lightly butter four individual pudding moulds.

Grind the walnuts in a liquidizer or food processor. Sift
the flour, baking powder and salt into a bowl and mix
in the ground walnuts.

Cream the butter, brown sugar and orange zest together
in a bowl until pale and fluffy. Gradually beat in the
eggs. Gently fold in the flour mixture until evenly
mixed; it should have a soft, dropping consistency.
Divide the mixture between the prepared pudding
moulds. Bake for about 25 minutes, until the puddings
are well risen and firm to touch.

While the puddings are baking, prepare the toffee sauce.
First, blanch the walnuts: place in a saucepan and cover
with cold water. Bring to the boil, then drain. Rub the
skins from the nuts, then chop roughly.

Place the caster sugar in a saucepan with 3 tablespoons
water. Heat gently until the sugar is dissolved, then
bring to the boil. Boil rapidly until the syrup becomes
a deep caramel colour. Quickly whisk the cream and
butter into the caramel. The sauce will be lumpy at first
but keep whisking – it will become smooth and glossy.
Stir the chopped walnuts into the sauce.

Carefully turn the puddings out on to serving plates.
Serve with the toffee sauce poured over, ideally with
a scoop of caramel ice cream.

*Pot-roasted duck with fresh figs and a watercress salad followed
by this pudding would make a lovely winter meal.*

MULLED PLUMS
with crème fraîche

SERVES 4

300 ml/10 fl oz soft red wine
   (e.g. Merlot)
100 ml/3 fl oz ruby port
pared zest of 1 lemon
2 cinnamon sticks, broken
   into 2 or 3 pieces
5 cloves
10 juniper berries
2–3 tablespoons unrefined
   molasses sugar
325g/12 oz dessert plums
3 teaspoons arrowroot

To serve
crème fraîche
a little ground cinnamon

Heat the wine and port in a saucepan and bring to the boil. Reduce the heat and add the lemon zest, cinnamon sticks, cloves, juniper berries and sugar. Leave to simmer steadily while you prepare the plums.

Wash, dry, halve and stone the plums.

In a small bowl, blend the arrowroot with 2–3 teaspoons cold water until smooth. Pour some of the hot wine over the arrowroot, stirring all the time. Return to the pan and cook until thickened and clear. Pour the hot wine mixture over the plums and leave to cool with all the aromatics. Store in the refrigerator overnight. The juices from the plums will add to the liquid.

Before serving, discard the cloves, lemon zest and cinnamon. The juniper berries can be left in for visual impact if you like. Serve in pretty glasses, with a separate bowl of crème fraîche dusted with cinnamon.

It's very difficult to follow outdoor barbecue food with a dessert, but I think these mulled plums with their aromatic flavours are just right.

The Basics

Vanilla custard

SERVES 4

600 ml/1 pint double cream
1 vanilla pod
5 egg yolks
1 teaspoon cornflour
1 tablespoon caster sugar

Put the cream into a saucepan. Split the vanilla pod in half lengthwise, scrape out the seeds into the cream and add the pod as well.

Whisk the egg yolks, cornflour and sugar together in a bowl.

Bring the cream to boiling point, then remove the vanilla pod. Allow the cream to rise in the pan, then quickly pour on to the egg mixture, whisking continuously until the mixture thickens.

Pour the custard through a fine sieve into a serving jug.

The cornflour should prevent the eggs from curdling. If you need to reheat the custard, do this very gently. Should it look like curdling at this stage, quickly whisk in a tablespoon of cold double cream.

Hazlenut shortbread fingers

MAKES 15–20

15g/½ oz hazelnuts

25 g/1 oz caster sugar

50 g/2 oz unsalted butter, at room
temperature

50 g/2 oz plain flour

25 g/1 oz semolina

To skin the hazelnuts and increase their flavour, spread them on a baking sheet and roast in a hot oven (190°C/375°F/Gas Mark 5) for 4–5 minutes, until the nuts are golden and the skins start to lift – do not let them burn. Tip on to one half of a clean dry tea towel. Fold the second half over the hot nuts and rub with the tea towel until the skins come off. Leave to cool completely, then chop finely.

Preheat the oven to 160°C/325°F/Gas Mark 3. Grease a baking sheet.

Cream the butter and sugar together in a bowl until pale and fluffy.

Sieve the flour and semolina together, add the nuts, then gradually work into the creamed mixture until it forms a dough. Finish the mixing with your hands, then gently knead the dough on a lightly floured surface until smooth. This is a fragile dough, so handle it lightly and carefully.

Roll out lightly to a rectangle about 5 mm/¼ inch thick. Cut it into fingers and transfer to the baking sheet. Crimp the edges with the back of a fork and make fork marks all over the dough in even lines; this helps to prevent the biscuits from bubbling up in places. Bake for 10–12 minutes, until lightly coloured. Dredge with caster sugar and leave on the baking sheet to cool (the biscuits become crisp when cold).

ORANGE SANDWICH CAKE

175 g/6 oz butter, softened
175 g/6 oz caster sugar
finely grated zest of 1 orange
175 g/6 oz self-raising flour
1 teaspoon baking powder
3 large eggs, beaten

Leave the butter to soften at room temperature for a few hours.

Preheat the oven to 160°C/325°F/Gas Mark 3. Butter two 20 cm/8 inch sandwich tins and dredge with caster sugar.

Sift the flour and baking powder together into a mixing bowl. Add the butter, sugar, orange zest and eggs and beat together with a balloon whisk until smooth and of a soft dropping consistency.

Divide the mixture between the prepared tins and bake for 20–25 minutes, until golden and firm in the middle. Turn out on to a wire rack and leave to cool.

PASTRY CREAM

300 ml/½ pint single cream
½ split vanilla pod
2 egg yolks
1 tablespoon plain flour
½ teaspoon cornflour
1 tablespoon caster sugar

Put the cream in a saucepan. Scrape the vanilla seeds into the cream, add the pod, then bring the cream to the boil. Blend the yolks, flour, cornflour and sugar in a bowl. Gradually pour the hot cream on to the yolks, whisking continuously. Rinse the pan and return the mixture to a low heat. Cook gently, stirring, until thickened. Remove the vanilla pod and cover with buttered greaseproof paper or clingfilm to prevent a skin forming.

TO CRYSTALLIZE ROSE PETALS

Prepare the crystallized petals several hours before you need them. Take the petals from the rose buds (or use small petals from the centre of an open rose) and leave to dry on paper towels for about 1 hour.

Paint the dry petals with lightly beaten egg white, using a clean artist's paintbrush – do not leave any blobs of egg white on the petals. Dredge with caster sugar from a fine dredger and leave on absorbent paper to dry out. The petals will become firm and crisp but retain their natural appearance.

The same technique can be used for any edible flowers such as borage, elderflowers or violets. Pick the flowers in the morning on a dry day and examine them carefully for insects before use.

Authors and titles

STARTERS
Jean Christophe Novelli Chef/patron of Maison Novelli, which opened in London to great acclaim in 1996. He previously worked at the Four Seasons restaurant, London.

VEGETABLE SOUPS
Elisabeth Luard Cookery writer for the *Sunday Telegraph Magazine* and author of *European Peasant Food* and *European Festival Food*, which won a Glenfiddich Award.

GOURMET SALADS
Sonia Stevenson The first woman chef in the UK to be awarded a Michelin star, at the Horn of Plenty in Devon. Author of *The Magic of Saucery* and *Fresh Ways with Fish*.

FISH AND SHELLFISH
Gordon Ramsay Chef/proprietor of one of London's most popular restaurants, Aubergine, recently awarded its second Michelin star. He is the author of *A Passion for Flavour*.

CHICKEN, DUCK AND GAME
Nick Nairn Chef/patron of Braeval restaurant near Aberfoyle in Scotland, whose BBC-TV series *Wild Harvest* was last summer's most successful cookery series, accompanied by a book.

LIVERS, SWEETBREADS AND KIDNEYS
Simon Hopkinson Former chef/patron at London's Bibendum restaurant, columnist and author of *Roast Chicken and Other Stories* and the forthcoming *The Prawn Cocktail Years*.

VEGETARIAN
Rosamond Richardson Author of several vegetarian titles, including *The Great Green Gourmet* and *Food from Green Places*. She has also appeared on television.

PASTA
Joy Davies One of the creators of *BBC Good Food Magazine*, she has been food editor of *She, Woman* and *Options* and written for the *Guardian, Daily Telegraph* and *Harpers & Queen*.

CHEESE DISHES
Rose Elliot The UK's most successful vegetarian cookery writer and author of many books, including *Not Just a Load of Old Lentils* and *The Classic Vegetarian Cookbook*.

POTATO DISHES
Patrick McDonald Author of the forthcoming *Simply Good Food* and Harvey Nichols' food consultant.

BISTRO COOKING
Anne Willan Founder and director of La Varenne Cookery School in Burgundy and West Virginia. Author of many books and a specialist in French cuisine.

ITALIAN COOKING
Anna Del Conte is the author of *The Classic Food of Northern Italy* (chosen as the 1996 Guild of Food Writers Book of the Year) and *The Gastronomy of Italy*. She has appeared on BBC-TV's *Masterchef*.

VIETNAMESE COOKING

Nicole Routhier One of the United States' most popular cookery writers, her books include *Cooking Under Wraps*, *Nicole Routhier's Fruit Cookbook* and the award-winning *The Foods of Vietnam*.

MALAYSIAN COOKING

Jill Dupleix One of Australia's best known cookery writers, with columns in the *Sydney Morning Herald* and *Elle*. Author of *New Food*, *Allegro al dente* and the Master Chefs *Pacific*.

PEKING CUISINE

Helen Chen Learned to cook traditional Peking dishes from her mother, Joyce Chen, the grande dame of Chinese cooking in the United States. The author of *Chinese Home Cooking*.

STIR FRIES

Kay Fairfax Author of several books, including *100 Great Stir-fries*, *Homemade* and *The Australian Christmas Book*.

NOODLES

Terry Durack Australia's most widely read restaurant critic and co-editor of the *Sydney Morning Herald Good Food Guide*. He is the author of *YUM!*, a book of stories and recipes.

NORTH INDIAN CURRIES

Pat Chapman Started the Curry Club in 1982. Appears regularly on television and radio and is the author of eighteen books, the latest being *The Thai Restaurant Cookbook*.

BARBECUES AND GRILLS

Brian Turner Chef/patron of Turner's in Knightsbridge and one of Britain's most popular food broadcasters; he appears frequently on *Ready Steady Cook*, *Food and Drink* and many other television programmes.

SUMMER AND WINTER CASSEROLES

Anton Edelmann Maître Chef des Cuisines at the Savoy Hotel, London, and author of six books. He appears regularly on BBC-TV's *Masterchef*.

TRADITIONAL PUDDINGS

Tessa Bramley Chef/patron of the acclaimed Old Vicarage restaurant in Ridgeway, Derbyshire. Author of *The Instinctive Cook*, and a regular presenter on a new Channel 4 daytime series *Here's One I Made Earlier*.

DECORATED CAKES

Jane Asher Author of several cookery books and a novel. She has also appeared in her own television series, *Jane Asher's Christmas* (1995).

FAVOURITE CAKES

Mary Berry One of Britain's leading cookery writers, her numerous books include *Mary Berry's Ultimate Cake Book*. She has made many television and radio appearances and is a regular contributor to cookery magazines.

Text © Tessa Bramley 1997

Tessa Bramley has asserted her right to be identified
as the author of this Work.

Photographs © Simon Wheeler 1997

First published in 1997 by
George Weidenfeld & Nicolson
The Orion Publishing Group
Orion House
5 Upper St Martin's Lane
London WC2H 9EA

British Library Cataloguing-in-Publication data
A catalogue record for this book is available from the
British Library

ISBN 0 297 82297 7

Designed by Lucy Holmes
Edited by Maggie Ramsay
Food styling by Joy Davies
Typeset by Tiger Typeset